Ravishing Europa

Other Books by Peter Robinson

Poetry
Overdrawn Account
This Other Life
Entertaining Fates
Lost and Found
About Time Too
Selected Poems 1976–2001
Ghost Characters
The Look of Goodbye
The Returning Sky
Buried Music
Collected Poems 1976–2016

Prose & Interviews
Untitled Deeds
Talk about Poetry: Conversations on the Art
Spirits of the Stair: Selected Aphorisms
Foreigners, Drunks and Babies: Eleven Stories
The Draft Will
September in the Rain
The Constitutionals

Translations
The Great Friend and Other Translated Poems
Selected Poetry and Prose of Vittorio Sereni
The Greener Meadow: Selected Poems of Luciano Erba
Poems by Antonia Pozzi

Criticism
In the Circumstances: About Poems and Poets
Poetry, Poets, Readers: Making Things Happen
Twentieth Century Poetry: Selves and Situations
Poetry & Translation: The Art of the Impossible
The Sound Sense of Poetry

RAVISHING EUROPA

PETER ROBINSON

worple
press

First published in 2019 by
Worple Press
Achill Sound, 2b Dry Hill Road
Tonbridge
Kent TN9 1LX.
www.worplepress.co.uk

Printed by imprintdigital
Upton Pyne, Exeter
www.imprintdigital.com

Typeset and cover design by narrator typesetters and designers
www.narrator.me.uk
info@narrator.me.uk
033 022 300 39

ISBN: 978-1-905208-43-2

Contents

One

'*Europe lies naked to their abuse—*'
Geoffrey Hill, *The Triumph of Love* (1998)

Belongings

'Les jours s'en vont je demeure'
Guillaume Apollinaire

Staying in Europe, as you do,
now on a train from Milan
we happen upon two Belgian girls
with strawberries, a ball of wool
and a copy of Apollinaire's *Alcools*
(one quotes 'Le pont Mirabeau');
two teenage girls off to see the world,
they're going as far as Istanbul.
So when our train makes Parma station,
we're wishing them a '*Bon vacance!*'
and they reply, '*You too!*'

Staying in Europe a week or two,
we're entranced by reddish leaves
when candy-floss blossoms envelope
this area's fragrant airs
and there's even a duck on the foul-
smelling flow of its old canal,
a lesser celandine
amidst the dandelions and daisies,
their meadow a greener green—
as if the in-two-minds of Europe
were fighting it out through you.

For despite the many money calculations,
scare-mongering or true, what's true
is we belong among these homes
(the popular housing of post-war years)

beyond a confetti of magnolia petals
scattered over mossy lawns
while some still cling to their garden boughs
in different or indifferent times…
and staying in Europe, as we intend to do.

3 April 2016

Monterosso

after Montale

The lemon trees, a place-name
and everywhere those fond quotations,
memories, our dead come
back like the clatter of a disappearing train
between its local station's
two tunnel mouths, the sense of shame
and a shame returning too
where, paused in foam, sun-fringed, the bathers pose...

Then it's as if we had come home
to ourselves once more, our shivering discoveries
of thirty years before
like swimmers in the glittering of their own waves;
and yet how changed now, crowds,
our faces crumpled in the warped cheval glass
or—a last example—Chinese
sightseers passing underneath his lemon trees!

Written in the Bay

'Too happy they, whose pleasure sought
Extinguishes all sense and thought
Of the regret that pleasure leaves,
Destroying life alone, not peace!'
Percy Bysshe Shelley

I sat and watched the tankers move
along a skyline, from a cove
where bathers and their children played
at swimming lessons. High waves made
inroads on the beach, salt water
reaching far enough to scatter
books, towels, mobile phones… which sank
with 'the regret that pleasure' [blank]
'leaves' is unlikely, maybe 'cease',
'destroying' or 'seeking life', 'not peace'.
Yes, peace… but the rest would have to be
rubbed out by that thoughtless sea.

Violated Landscape

From heights at Portovenere
by Byron's grotto where the bay
opens out towards Lerici,
there in spray-gunned, cursive script,
white, on a high metallic screen
paesaggio violentato were the words
and, finally, it dawned on me
what they couldn't help but mean:

the screen concealed a real eyesore
in the shape of a Liberty-style hotel,
its khaki-coloured plasterwork
flaking off the raw brick courses;
shutters half closed on dust-plumed suites,
the whole thing sheathed in scaffolding
as for WORKS IN PROGRESS
but rusted from the salt sea air…

It's been here thirty, forty years.
Whatever the graffiti-poet meant
subtitling this rapturous view
seen again on a fine spring day,
those breezes filled yacht-racing sails
under the Apuan and Apennine chains.
Cloud convoys rose above their snow.
And we were as carried away by it too.

Ravishing Europa

for O

After staying up, oh, far too late
for a televised debate
and sickened at the bickering,
I'm reminded of Europa
by some more mendacious bullshit—
then gone to bed, succumb
again to sorry memories…
They bring back lying with the victim
of a far-off rape, a
ravishing, like the ones depicted
in occidental summer twilight
on its sunset lands.

Still now you haver round our bedroom;
me, I'm undecided whether
it had been an act of love
or violence provided
the very idea, to try the patience
of Europa, send her home…
But oh, deciding for us
despite the Cretan myths, the liars,
here you are beside me—
and I can only hope
it's like we're in the arms of Europe
with Europe in my arms.

May 2016

Lincolnshire Landscapes

for Peter Makin

'... *there is a constant sense, as in a Dutch landscape,*
of how the road leads on beyond the visible horizon.'
Richard Wollheim

1

Farmed deer—they're venison under rain—
bound off on their balletic points;
but we're about to lose our way
with a box-pew church ahead,
its east end silhouetted
up against rain-laden sky—
the pockmarked, ochre stonework bitten
in by centuries of frost.

2

Under big skies of the Lincolnshire Wolds
when driven down field-skirting roads,
I'm grateful for that constant sense
of how they lead beyond
the visible horizon, land
moved across our windscreen frame,
our windscreen smeared by summer's extinctions;
it's shot through with reflections,
the overlaid experience
as if sands rippling along a shore...

3

the shore by Mablethorpe, for instance,
with its razor-shells, hundreds and thousands,
and wind, wind speaking in tongues
of streaming sands—
wraiths blown towards a steely sea
break, break, breaking under iron-grey cloud forms,
where figures, patterns on that beach,
point off beyond more ghost propellers;
over towards the Wash they reach,
or Humber estuary.

4

Leaving the big red VOTE LEAVE signs
behind us in a homeward turn,
we find the B-roads leading on to
abandonment, abjection, where it will have them choose;
it's figured in those FOR SALE boards,
and what of language, person, coast
emerges now we are to lose
ourselves beyond the turning lines
from that last horizon…

Balkan Trilogy

in memory of Geoffrey Hill

'prega per Europa'
Vittorio Sereni

1. Passport Stamps

There's something about those rock outcrops
along the tops above Dubrovnik,
bloodied, fallen oranges
in the moat around what was Ragusa—
something about a switchback mountain
road that leads inland
(mist rising from a reservoir lake
after temperature-changing rain;
bridge pillars emerging from it
as if from out of nowhere)—
something about an exclamation-mark road sign
when we cross more Dayton borders
and the words
switch back and forth between Roman and Cyrillic—
there's something can't but point towards
past damage, harms to come...

2. Nikšić Hotel

Like a convalescent from this month of claim
and counter-claim, I falter
coming down to breakfast, seeing as the same
worn carpet would soon alter

when overwhelmed by risen shame
I find no shelter
from the Montenegrin sun's heat, or from casting blame
in a welter
of muffled shouts, disorientation,
hearing news that wrecks it—
plain omelette, bread and tea become
tasteless as the one word *nation*…
Not knowing where to turn for home,
I return to my room through the door marked EXIT.

3. Herceg Novi

As at a bereavement, when those harms
from your loss are falling
into place with relief like some more evening breeze,
under the prom's transplanted palms
beside seafront concessions
there come, among raucous darts of starlings
at dusk above the old town's eaves,
sensible inward migrations…
So from a balcony, soon after sunrise,
no less at home here, you see
spectral headlands jut into isolated sea
and can hardly believe your eyes.

June 2016

Garden Thoughts

'mi pareva di essere in Europa'
Luciano Erba

At this hour, they well may be
watering gardens throughout Europe,
but beyond a misted window
our front-garden patch
has an air of strangeness (though
Japanese anemones,
foxglove bells and fuchsias
hedged round by box in disarray
could look thus any year);

now through this miserable June
when the dwarf pine thrusts up taller
and a tumbling acer
fills out her underskirts,
raindrops flicker in the puddles
adding globules and a gleam
to droop-headed flowers—
like they too want their country back,
and it's not coming home.

Bibliographical Note

'Es war ein Traum.'
Heinrich Heine

for Derek Slade

I dreamed last night, or the night before,
how a poem of mine
unexpectedly appeared in some little magazine
whose pages fell out on the floor—

for this publication had the strangest of styles:
its format's ragged margin
formed the entire, the sceptred coastline
of our British Isles.

In the Apennines

after Eric Newby

Even the sunflowers look depressed
as we drive towards those hills...
Bent, desiccated, they no longer turn
petals crazed with light to any sun;
and talk, too, touches on downturns
in the market price for wheat
now this region's pasta-making firms
won't buy local either.

Yet eyes still gaze to the fields of hill farms,
their turned earth dry, as low sun warms
familiar curves, and our holiday-
season brings the families out to eat
grilled meat in these mountains.

Precipitous views to far crests would start
ever more distant memories
of things dads said about those years:
what happened at Torrechiara
or Berchetto where the Germans were,
a granddad in black-tasseled fez
among the disappeared...

But now sky softens to a cloud-flecked blue
I think of you hidden from war's alarms,
harms and excursions hereabouts,
who came back after to find your love
and did, and married her—

to think of it here, as, relaxed outside,
we've formed a wider family circle
and the recent generation's
minx-like three-year-old Eva runs
now to one, now to another's arms.

Women of Elche

for Maria Consuelo Tenas & Isabel Vila Vera

I

Because what the sentinel palm tree sees
or white factory's single brick chimney
might be that low gleam, warm
beyond the town oases—
and because these blank developments
in sombre arable land,
a pueblo-like farmstead
surviving before more new concessions,
seem stage sets for a future
which through interminable crises
wouldn't come to pass—
'I can't continue,' as she said,
in a passion with our tired friend
and meaning that the politics
would leave her lost for words
among labyrinthine franchising outlets,
roundabouts, stoplights, sunset's boulevards...

2

'I mustn't complain though,' our friend said
though overworked, exhausted,
because many don't have even that;
they're compelled to emigrate
from this desert-like, desiccated place
with its brackish waters

where the Caliphate of Cordoba
ordered an oasis—
and because those salt tears filled her eyes
when from the Valley of Jehoshaphat
during their miracle play's
Death and Assumption there came
an annual surprise
hidden behind the sky's
pale-blue-painted dome, a palm
descending out of Paradise.

Plaza de las Monjas

'Ceremos pronto las fronteras

…

Un fantasma recorre Europa'
Rafael Alberti

for Antonio Orihuela

Dusk is warming the house-fronts' whitewash.
Under a stone column, topped by a bust
(that's Christopher Columbus gazes westwards),
here come voices sounding words.

On a nunnery belfry, etched by slant light,
words stretch towards its vast stork's nest;
they reach up to those sunset swifts
acrobatic through aerials' attenuated blue.

★

There's an under-murmur of children playing
that goes on late into the night;
but now those voices rise above it
calling out so-called crisis, loss…

and the people who then happen by
from a convent, a wedding, or Africa,
hearing them, are curious,
might join in with the long applause.

★

19

Hernandez reciting to his lost volunteers!
And it's as if I were among them
in a far memory of that photo
(although stone-deaf in my right ear).

I'm listening for some future music,
Zukunftsmusik, oh Europe, Europe,
which might be even farther off now
or, at least, not getting nearer.

★

Hang-dog, collarless, bitten by fleas,
strays are barking without let-up
about extremities of Europe
as at Montenegro, at Moguer...

They follow us to get adopted,
bound on down an empty street
loping in and out of shadow
or yap at sirens through this sullen heat.

★

We attend to them, still strain towards
remote, forever taunting echoes
from consequences, unforeseen,
in fierce complaints, those sounds of words

on background sounds, not going away;
we're listening for some much-neglected
rhythm in what you or I might say
because we too were the future once!

★

20

But now in this plaza's lemon trees
paired black, cast-iron lamps begin
to flicker with, first, a lime-green glow,
then steady as that paler yellow;

and through the dark voices continue
attenuated, too, at these extremes—
while Christopher Columbus still looks on,
expectant, towards his gone-down sun.

Moguer (Huelva), 30 July 2016

On a Walk to Sonning

'If you believe you're a citizen of the world,
you are a citizen of nowhere.'
Theresa May, 5 October 2016

What with all the unacceptable faces
in group portraits of an era,
their demonic industries

for a *carpe diem* or a *sauve qui peut*,
words of another vicar's daughter
are urging us to 'seize the day'—

★

which we do now on a walk to Sonning
in earliest autumn, while our talk's
of children raised in other countries,

both their parents aliens there,
third-culture kids' grass roots, a tree's
torn at by the air…

★

For everyone's got to be somewhere:
on undermining subsidence
in fracked Lancashire, for instance,

their real, their local *amor loci*, mine,
whether a flagpole, or mown lawn,
or forlorn estate…

★

Yes, everyone's got to be somewhere:
when flown above Siberian wastes,
through cloudscapes of a Baltic day

or stuck in traffic, at a stop-light
as only space crawls on forever,
peace talks are in disarray,

★

we're vulnerable transients, all of us,
so near yet far off littorals,
Europe's shores on which to lodge—

or rescued from the mid-sea waves
in need of shelter, safe house, home,
and who are you to judge?

Out of Europe

'Tell me again about Europe and her pains'
William Empson

to Rosemary Laxton

Now another ghost from Europe
summoned by historic grief
and grievance, you have come,
a ghost I didn't recognize
travelling this far
to congratulate or criticize,
a ghost I had such feelings for
despite what age and damage shape.

No, no, you've not forgotten
how such a one's salvation
could be another's purgatory
made of things said, things written,
bringing small relief—
as if formed sound and sense
reshaping what was done
can never make a difference.

Which is why it had to be
on yet another rainy
night in a different September, a shy
gesture, almost of *hello*,
makes it seem the past you are,
haunting Broad Street's shop-front shadow,
has returned this far
to wave a chance goodbye.

The Prospects

for Tom Phillips

1

Dark amazon striding towards us
across a dockland swing-bridge,
she's not afraid of two grey beards
deep in conversation—
and nor's the café-terrace waitress
with her 'How is everything?'
as we wonder what might be amiss
below a coaster's moored black stern.

2

Despite the burned-out petrol station
and demolition site we pass,
everything's plain in an off-scape ahead
as you talk about the docks
amongst its storied populations
remaining, yes, remainiacs
from this seaport's field full of folk,
trade-winded migratory stocks.

3

Plain too, your plan to emigrate
cutting through developments
far as where prospects are barred
under the pastel terraces;

for wanting to remain you'll leave
and, leaving, they have to remain
while the very air's free movement is
still cleaving to such heresies.

Sonning Lock

This year's reed-growths in autumn, faded
chevrons pointing off downstream,
recall them while the skein of water
alters level in slow time—
its ripples, lifeless, muddy, dark
(as painted by a Stanley Spencer),
recall them when the strain
of taking one more aeroplane
between our embassies descends—
recall the brick lock-keeper's house,
the date a century ago,
yes, built in the same year as the Somme
by Thames Conservancy—
recall it when your demagogues assume
'the people' and 'the people's will',
when much-used words only mean themselves—
and listen who's from nowhere now
in that diplomatic chill.

World Citizens

for Matilde & Giulia

As at Verne Point, above the curves
of breakwater piers, wide harbour walls,
with Weymouth Bay below, its waves
flecked by Sunday dinghy sails
tacking about, and Chesil Beach
disappearing off into a haze,
I *have* felt foreign everywhere—

★

been driven away from a thing like home
to earn my living, raise children, love
like others do, and come back too,
to so much dereliction—
this see-through concrete honeycomb's
eyesore of unfinished rooms
(more long abandoned speculation),

★

and to your words much less than fair
on UK passport holders, those
with other languages and friends
in different time zones, not bereft
of anywhere, your spoken words
for these the policies had left
behind, as on steep-sloped estates—

★

since first you drove them to despair,
then used resentments, rage
for a coup and putsch... Now, here,
wave-lines are faintly vorticized
along this seaweed-reeking beach
cross-cut by groynes at Swanage;
more seaside surrealist ordinary life,

★

it's like an insomniac's nightmare.

Die Holzwege

'*das Auge des N[ihilisten]… das Untreue*
übt gegen seine Erinnerungen—es läßt sie
fallen, sich entblättern'
Friedrich Nietzsche

1

These wooded paths like arguments
about belonging here have rents
shot through with leaf-stopped rays
and shady undergrowth, tired ways
in a world of airborne ills where,
detached, we're able still to care
that Dutch elm, dieback, acid rain
find the woods in trouble…

2

Then shivered fronds' foxed fringes
start awe in our ordinary exchanges
about more loss, and memories
like the leaves on deciduous trees
fall naturally…

3

As even belonging's tainted now our
advocates of being, their will to power,
have appropriated woodland paths
leaving us autumn's aftermaths;

you asked me if that beech was dead,
but I supposed it must have shed
leaves early from its shrivelled rust
carpeting...

4

And how the tree survives on trust!

Night Flight

'The time had come for him to
set out on his journey westward.'
James Joyce, 'The Dead'

1

From out a faint mist, to Ireland I come
through the black rift or gash
and find a mild autumn,
its entire green canopy of tones on the turn:
as though Gabriel Conroy's wish
in all that general snow
for a continental holiday
had been granted at last
and the nearest way to Europe, now,
were this going west.

2

Well met at Shannon by their John or Seán,
an ex-lorry-driver who tells me
what he knows about crossing a border
(hard as that could be),
well, sure, now I'm all ears
on the quiet roads towards Limerick—
old garrison town with its castle and wharves
where we're as welcome as you like
in our common travel area's
flurrying of orange-tinged leaves on the turn.

3

Deposited at Castletroy and come
like an old man to this country,
I may stroll at ease
above the Shannon's dark mutinous waves
into County Clare, then back again,
might dream or live in hope;
and from one end of Europe
where the same arts must maintain
an understanding, peace,
can stare up at those tones in mild autumn.

Post-Truth

Now this year's word's a tribute
to the thing it leaves behind,
or thinks to do, mistakenly;

for truth is like a Lazarus
rising from its grave-clothes
to judge each diverse ruse.

2016

Two

'Ich bemerkte, dass ich mitten in Europa stand.'
Yoko Tawada, *Wo Europa Anfängt* (1991)

Bloomsbury Way

for Giulia

With violins sounding still in your head
on Marchmont Street or Southampton Row,
Giulia, I think of you
living the life I'd have loved to have led—
your glimpses of pellucid sky
past glass façades and cliff-like stone
or in Queen Square, sun gone down,
that old mind hospital, the one I worked at,
swathed in sheeting for a facelift or what
with *sviolinate* of my own
following the streets and street corners.

Oh no, not lost again, you know
this time, you know
where you are going and what you are doing;
by rose garden statues, memorial benches,
leaves a dark canopy suspended in air,
Giulia, you're leading me
to the *Marquis Cornwallis* or else *Ciao Bella*
while London's slotted dusks will colour
flakes of cloud across void spaces
as mementos to these mindful places—
Museum Street or Foster Court's
fresh associations…

With violins sounding no less loud now
on Marchmont Street or Southampton Row,
how tears come, uncontrollable,
for the lost pasts, missed futures

by Tube stations where you canvassed to remain:
from geographies of identity,
your theme, now, borne in mind
on these so much more world-filled streets
where the city is you,
you're the city,
you, love.

The Hard and Soft of It

1

Unforeseen snowdrops spot mud verges,
banks of them, and carpet copses
through countryside as fear
of trespass gets the better of us
out where loneliness clarifies
nothing towards North Sea horizons;
and, look, its wind-farm turbines
are ready for our Don Quixotes
as they appear and disappear
in a misted depth of air...

2

where grey-and-white spots de-abstractify
to seagulls in cloud-crossed pools
surrounded by broad ochre sand-stripes;
each stratified, perceptual plane
de-abstractifies, now, before our eyes
to derelict wayside hostelries
nobody could make a go of, gone
along trunk roads from the coast and, sure,
they are welcome to more lost past
if they'll spare us a bit of snatched future!

Drawing a Line

Walking Man (1950)

Resilient squirrel with your dropped takeaway
on a Denis Lasdun precipice,
there's no need to freeze, though fazed by this,
because, entranced, I'll let you be—

me moving over a glass-sided walkway
like some *ad hoc* Giacometti
attenuated, kneaded sculpture-piece
striding through the day.

Still Life (1949)

Forgive me, café-au-lait-coloured pigeon,
still as you like on a grey concrete wall,
you rabbits at your breakfasting
off these central reservations—

because we're located, here in framed spaces,
as if one of his much-hatched sketches
on which each figure's found its own
ground and outline in the phased approximations.

The Tree (1949)

But—wind through the tree—forgive me my dismay.
I only heard you sighing
as eyes closed on broad water's edges
and strollers cooled their feet from landing stages.

Then here was DANGER, ground suddenly shelving,
on a glorious day, as that architect called it,
when warm, uninterrupted sunshine
would draw such creatures from their habitats and home.

The Vehicle

1. Taxi

Pre-dawn, a taxi draws up outside.
It's a black Mercedes ride.
Its driver loads our overweight baggage
and in darkness pulls away.
The spring still at an early stage,
we're bound to miss magnolia
blossom blustered down Crescent Road
now that April's almost here;
we're bound to miss the English spring
rough with hoary dew this year—
pulling away from every last thing
including our most dear.

2. Shame

Away this early, there's barely a soul
on still-sleeping streets around
and not much traffic at this hour,
nor fear of missing planes;
but past that roundabout flyover spur
linking us with the M4
suddenly a shame, the shame
of leaving, leaving comes again
by slip-road and littered hard shoulder
on our equivocal ride.

3. The Letter

Just two days after her letter's delivered
you see we're leaving too,
passing a turn-off for Maidenhead
(the bridge where Turner's hare is chased
forever by the future in *Rain, Steam and Speed*).
There respect for 'the will of the people'
and ends of a political career
may briefly, when May follows, coincide
on our sorrow-laden ride…

4. Left Behind

We're leaving behind for a four-month leave
great dark warehouse skeletons
like the Gaumont or like Johnson's dye-works
as if her citizens of nowhere—
us, with our burdened-down baggage
in which though humbled, belittled,
left behind by the passages of time,
here's my dad's first vicarage
surviving it—their non-benign neglect,
years' ruin, the abject entities
instanced in dark field-edge trees
we're passing on our ride.

5. Darkness

Now Eton's gone, and Windsor too.
Stark crosstrees thickening over hedgerows,
their capillary branches splay
as through this Cimmerian pre-dawn
our taxi plunges on
and pollarded trees' bare, ruined boughs
are blackened, angled remnants
jaggedly poking at a lightless sky—
like staring into that heart of darkness
before us
       where illusion and self-interest ally.

6. Terminal

But then our black-bile-coloured taxi
pulls up outside of Terminal 3.
I've tipped the driver for this inspiration:
a manifesto, one more of our lost causes,
words find, humiliated, left behind
in this trolley baggage, voices
packed with meanings, sorrow-laden,
now the contradictions would pull us all to pieces
and you, you bear that in mind.

31 March 2017

Where Europe Ends

'*qui non siamo in Europa,*
siamo in Portogallo.'
Antonio Tabucci, *Sostiene Pereira*

Look here, among the merchants' houses
at Kobe with their imitation
hair-styles and tooth powders...

or underneath the Sannomiya
railway arch, by each arcade shop,
while I courier an envelope
(it's sealed, not to be opened)
containing a criminal record report
from the Hyogo Police Department;

or at your Italian Consulate
where the thing's to be translated
in aid of a passport application,
and I'll suffer that vertiginous glass-walled lift
plunging from an umpteenth floor
with the nothing it revealed—

★

or in the Expo ethnology museum's
labyrinth collections;
alone amongst donated things,
there I found the Europe section's
illustrative items

include a painted Dutch organ on wheels,
the snapshots of our mountain sheep-farmers
and plaques about its 'changing face'
thanks to the inward migrations
of human transhumance—

because towards this end of Europe
it's like a William Adams
and his progeny would come home,
like imploding exploration
meant, as it says, 'the tide has turned',
and now their great experiment
promising to lose what we can't share
must open arms to everyone.

But in its courtyard's hieratic stair
are preserved those 'cheerful graves',
their 'relics of a future'.

★

Or else at Moscow airport
circa nineteen eighty-nine,
gone past a *Welcome to Europe* sign...

that's when I caught a glimpse of Yeltsin
beside some empty shelving
while our Sabina flight refueled,
and from its transit lounge's warmth
could see a man in uniform
stationed on the tarmac;
he wanted to come in from the cold,
would stamp, and clap his gloves.
Though there was nothing to desire,

they did take credit cards.
Then, at last, they took the boarding cards,
off-handed, let us go
on towards convertible currencies
over versts and wastes of snow.

★

My ear and eye affections
contracted in those elsewheres
with smatterings of languages
as if a rash, a skin disease,
have likewise disinclined me
to take things at face value.

Still, when she asked me did I think English
were the language for these places
lived in fourteen years,
it was like my words wouldn't stick to things
because not spoken there—
or if uttered by non-native speakers
would bring out inner distances
of de-familiarity!

But especially when back home here,
home, after four months away,
for there are gaps in our map of Europe
now glimpses of expressive features
leak anger, mute resentments
on the point of spilling into words,
the verbal tics, officious gestures
overcast and changeable
as an English summer's day.

★

In a bleak July or washed-out August
jet-lag morning, who are you
coming from another dreamscape
to start and startle me?

Who are you with these collages,
perpetual other woman,
still the same, and recognized,
although this time you've changed your hair?
An artist? Your *Merzbau* exhibit's
mounted like a low relief
that alters as it's gazed on now
among the crowd at a private view.

Have you been modeled from the life,
though composite? Somebody lost?
Someone I had to say goodbye to?
Or are you from that other England,
a country welcoming of strangers?
We plan to meet… you disappear…
then I'm left here to find you
in a washed-out August or late bleak July?

★

For it's like there is no end of Europe,
like I take it everywhere—
as if it were some scented soap
or that Mackintosh ladder-back chair…

Not distant from Dynevor Road (an instance)
where Joseph Conrad would return,
writing—as he did—the word Home
always means these hospitable shores

—and I'd come to recuperate
after nearly dying
to a nondescript, domestic street;
or else by Foscolo's emptied tomb
at Chiswick Cemetery,
the poet's shade no less '*più qui*'
in this time-desecrated, this exilic retreat...

Oh Europe, a young woman's wide-eyed features,
wind-strewn locks and coronet
on the back of a haulage company truck,
how you cover those inner distances,
come with me everywhere!

The Further Losses

'Tudo era irreparável.'
Carlos Drummond de Andrade

1. Bar Guareschi

Under an August bank holiday's
almost cloud-free skies
in the dead heart of a summer we'd come
here to Verdi's birthplace
but chanced upon the world of Don Camillo:
there were hardly-stirring trees
and background sounds of leaves, cicadas,
his laughter for a common good...
We found the sun-stunned village street
led on across flat, funded farmland
to nothing but the faint hills' profiles
and whatever was thus lost there in its haze.

2. Bar Ligabue

Those quiet towns below sea level
under a terra-plain of the Po,
Borretto's cupola and lido
or Gualtieri on a day's
outing beyond Brescello,
they have their own dazed fascination
for anyone inclined to gaze
off across that fertile farmland—
recessive, now, as on a canvas

by one of their local naïf-school painters
and be asked: do I miss them too?

3. Via Cimitero

Then it was as if Don Camillo himself
led the responses, glancing around
to check who among us would mouth those words
commending a poor soul to her God,
with bricklayer ready to wall up the ashes
after all is done and said—
which was how, in the presence of everyone,
we let the dead bury our dead!

4. La Forza del Destino

Protected, now, from speculation,
he's suffering a second death
in this silence, the unsaid,
and, no, I couldn't hear a thing
noticing those black-edged posters
pasted up around church doors
above another radio
tuned to an Italian station,
its latest news of migrant crises
broadcast through a loggia window—
for at this isolated point,
diminishing, which is the world,
I'm not allowed to speculate
on why he did away with it
by opting for that operatic fate.

5. After Poussin

Then under boughs beside the lake
it's like I was the one 'recoiling',
his gaze aghast, arms flailing
in *Landscape with a Man Killed by a Snake*;
it's like I'd looked into the face of death
and felt the soul squeezed from me too
by a serpent, that plain *memento
mori*, or symptom of the simple truth
despoiled by unjust accusations
now that it has come to this—
the gesture of those inscribed publications
twisted, turned into a damaged good,
when the only possible happiness
were in expressing gratitude.

6. At Calestano

And I know we've got to give time time
to work its level best—
but reading how the bombs aimed at a bridge
missed and hit this village
reported on a plaque at Calestano,
the grievances and grieving of our wars
incised for future memory
in Guernica's sixtieth anniversary year,
me, I can't help but fear
the iconoclasts, custodians in league
against nostalgias for a future
have done their worst, their damnedest…

7. La Villetta

But the earth's so rich it's good as oiled
and houses in clear air at sunset
might be the distances we've travelled,
oh, not to wake up old, but see
those later flashes of heat lightning
above towns' amber light pollution;
they glow as if beside tomb photos,
a parent's, friend's 'eternal flame'
still burning through our cemetery.

8. Bar Europa

These lowlands famous for their fogs,
they're hiding age-old fears
through winters when the distances
are blanked out by glaucoma blurs—
like an old man praying to depart in peace,
us edging over junctions
near Giuseppe Verdi Airport
to meet a homebound plane…
But now both flight and man are gone,
we stare across the fêted plain
towards whatever's lost in that haze,
while elsewhere politicians
on their holidays
are looking to the conference season
when there'll be yet more to get done.

Saudades da Europa

after Antonio Tabucci

1

Sweet-sorrowful memories of someone dear:
you find them come in waves
to a cliff-edge where the sea-swell purls...
We're queuing down steps at Riomaggiore
onto its short pier.
A ferryboat's balancing the mobile gangway,
and while it disembarks I hear
voices of all over Europe
heading, perhaps, for the Via d'Amore;
exclamatory murmurs, they climb up past us—
us waiting on our embarkation
to meet, imagine, Cytherea.

2

Sadness produced by the absence of loved objects:
as when the ravishing sun's decline
is set to throw all Portovenere in shade;
then later navigation across this bay
will be saying goodbye on waves of August breeze
as a vast container ship, laden high,
suddenly gives a hoot
with its pilot boat passing us by
like a guide, an idea...

3

or else melancholy caused by some lost good:
when a newly-varnished fishing craft,
bucking, struggles in our wake
and marinas' thick mast-forests come
with sunset like to test it
at the very last moment of a drawn-out day;
then the future loss of what's before us
steals like that nostalgia
as a soundtrack for our landing
drifts towards La Spezia
if you have, that is, eyes to see or ears to hear.

At this Distance

1

Arranging to meet at another private view,
she's here once again, the love of your night
in a scrambled Amsterdam, an Oterloo …

2

Unpredictably often, old too, this love comes
back as her series of dreamscapes to blame
or, elsewhere in Europe, disclaim you.

3

Like last night, no, not reunited in Heaven,
she and her clan were explaining the remnants
of reason enough, fair enough, to shame you!

4

But still, as a cooling tower's up-plumed steam
joins the cloud cover, she'll claim you
(even if at this distance, and only a dream).

Last Refuge

*'They say patriotism is the last refuge
to which a scoundrel clings...'*
Bob Dylan, after Dr. Johnson

High above the River Avon
here where tribal dialects
meet in another double naming
on Tory (no, from *tor*: a hill),
we're ravished by their gardens'
autumn-tinted schemes
of berry-red, the turning greens,
and now by sunbursts' glittering
on roadways from the town—
a strip of rain-reflected brightness
or brilliant way to go...

But, no, it's not that easy.
In their Saxon church porch
we find an old parishioner
dusting, and she tells me,
being all fear and prayer—
tells me how she's anxious
about our 'interesting times';

and oh our interesting times,
they're falling like the shadow cast
by topiary graveyard yews
amongst these storied hills
now it's falling to the likes of us
in our poorer, dear lifetimes
to relieve a country's ills
from its patriotic scoundrels.

Cold Comfort

'... *che ogni estremo di mali un bene annunci.*'
Umberto Saba, 'Poesia'

1

In the chilly blue-clear and dazzling light
of a late November, eyes
are squinting at its brightness—
a lucid luminosity
startling those rooflines;
mid-air, above the street, it shines
like a thing amongst us in this city
casting sharp-edged shadows
to divide the faces at a pavement café.
How an *ad hoc* chiaroscuro's trans-valuing our day!

2

It's the sort of thing my dad would say
'... that each extreme of ill announced a good',
which may well have rubbed off on me
for in all likelihood
scratch and you'll touch an optimist
(oh have it your own way,
you who like your comfort cold!)
and that's why I'm taking the blindness of now
to rummage for some signs we might have missed.

The Irish Border

'... one advantage of a farm that, as they say, bestrides
the border...'
Paul Muldoon

1

Through windswept, bare housing estates
past tree-less open spaces
where outrage, murder,
they would plan and order,
explaining, he toured me around
then sped away, the years come back to mind
when a white-flagged priest would still tread forward
in faded footage onto open ground
on any Sunday, bloody Sunday—
and how could they ever feel properly at home
with that camouflaged foot patrol
drawing a bead beside their garden gnome?

2

Still now, at least there's been an accord,
an end of the beginning, a back-stop,
another paper-scrap brought home from Europe
and announcing there won't be
any hard border on the island of Ireland:
the British government has given its word.

3

But, hold on, if there cannot be
a border in the Irish Sea,
can there be one beyond Calais?
And would you relocate the Jungle
beside old checkpoint parishes?
Better ask the DUP...

4

And not forgetting that schoolmate of mine
who back in the early Seventies
would supplement his summer-job pay
smuggling illicit contraceptives
for their right to life on a Saturday night
from Holyhead to Dún Laoghaire.

5

Ah but now, you've really got a nerve
saying they'll weaponize the border,
as though not fortified before...
and if you will call it a Trojan Horse,
well, the omens aren't propitious –
not to mention her ravishment that caused *that* war.

6

Filtered through leaves at an early window,
a flickering light in May,
at last, it might come home to you
Europe's a scapegoat, an alibi,
for the anger and grief leaving couldn't relieve,
shipping such consequences, unforeseen,
into the cold snows of a dream
when blessed are the peacemakers
for they shall see all manner of things!

Wall-to-Wall

'Alla fine solo la poesia può salvare l'Europa'
Cees Nooteboom, *La repubblica* 12 Dec 2015

1

A car windscreen opaque with leaves,
the pavements' brick and bricolage
or plane-tree-like, these flaked façades
backlit by storm- and sunlight,
they're in need of some renovating care—

2

such as given to a blue, adopted wall
with its Dutch word-cloud poem,
Jan Hanlo's, and in two translations:
als melk / als leem, like milk / like loam
or *kato mlyako / i kato zemya*—
where it's like those words had come
to weigh and find us wanting, wanting
a home in this chilly middle Europe…
It's as if his lines might save and spare.

3

Ah then the rashes of tagged graffiti,
sourced quotations *('to be or not to be')*
stenciled over its junction boxes
might mean, just so, you've got a hope
here on the yellow brick cobbles of Sofia.

Don Quixote in Sofia

'y lo que seria peor, hazerse poeta, que segun
dizen, es enfermedad incurable, y pegadiza.'
Miguel Cervantes

1. Fish Tank

Accordion-band arpeggio and near-full moon
float up above hard-liquor-advert neon
now that stray character, kept in a cupboard,
striped lance sticking out onto the floor space,
he's swelling to be glimpsed at distance
lit by branched lamps in the autumn trees;
through twilight on Vitosha Boulevard
its namesake mountain's cake-iced in snow,
La Mancha so very far away...

2. Drowned

Like the ghost of a father's political illusion
here he comes, tilting, and stumbling on,
incorrigible dad or a thwarted son...
Skeletally thin, with ghastly grey goatee,
off he drifts down by the Palace of Culture
(its EU-backed renewal works-in-progress)
to be tossed forever between those tyrannies
under different yokes, and this one of money's
into which he's all but gone.

On the Electricity

in memory of Tom Raworth

1

Something's wrong with our bathroom light.
'… all the immortality we have', I read
in words by Alexander Shurbanov,
and immediately the bulb flickers off;

or, another time, words from Osip Mandelstam,
'the unknown soldier's laid / In his famous grave'
when exactly that same fault happens, the same,
as if it were trying to tell me something.

2

Then, again, like those 'Ironic points of light'
flashed across Auden's dark, now ours,
an attic window's on–off opposite
sends its Morse-code message to the stars.

Three

'... *inquadrati nella storia di nostro Paese, che*
non li esclude dal loro posto di cittadini Europei.'
Eugenio Montale, 'Stile e tradizione' (1925)

This Last Year

Between those Alps and Apennines
on a walk towards the Po,
there are tall, spaced, roadside poplars,
planted fields of silver birch…
At sunset, here, church cupolas
interrupt surrounding darkness
streaked with red hopes for good weather;
but then a so-called super moon
emerges from horizon trees—
their fragile threads of branches
like violent scratch-marks on a ruddy face.

We're threading through an after dusk
along the wide, slow-flowing river,
are lost in conversation
on wherever best to live
late days, or else discreetly wonder
about a greener charm in distance
on the far bank's fertile side,
or at whatever may appear
over deepened skylines this last year.

Higher, whiter, blurred in mist
floated from warm earth, that moon
might be the common coinage
of our coming separation—
but breaking up is hard to do,
and the best part's even harder
now migrants go on envying
rights to be taken at the border
closing ahead as we pace on.

Ahead, through twilight, can you see
outlines of their fainting country?
Where, next year, they'll good as tell you
not to lament that loss of value
others envy? Abandon rage, outrage
at shames come from a muddy spring?
And why? Because, sans everything,
you'll reach that other country, age?

2 January 2018

Leave to Remain

'als nichtexistent im Eigen-Sinn
bürgerlicher Konvention...'
Christian Morgenstern

1

Wind-rushed seed, despondent
profiles on the tainted air
are driven by austerities,
a planned 'hostile environment'
where maple leaf and pine
stand up against a sky's
cloud cover, like despair—
which might as well be mine
along these parkland pathways
walking back to work again.

2

A plastic glass, a beer can,
wine boxes, fast food trays
are signs of more strayed revelries;

our young's consumer choices
lie decidedly abandoned
in the morning grass...

69

3

and that tree would have to come down.
Because a deathliness inside
turned its leaves too early brown

trucks rutted up the ground,
men wood-chipped lopped boughs
and left a stump behind.

4

But these, they were to leave
as the trees' re-leafing
aggravates a love
of home and, like them, striving

I had followed the money
to live as an alien,
though not without any
leave to remain—

dependent on officialdom
or shredded paperwork,
and with each unjust accusation
more damage could be done.

5

Although you might have known
'value for money' would be
another money value,
still, that something rotten tree-

trunk remains around
like a last memento,
a symbol or a symptom—
of words still tainting air back home.

6

Border controls already
at my office door,
today I have to scan a passport
should you want to read your poem,

then report on my Tier 4
Visa holders' meetings with me
if they're not to be sent home.

7

Oh European citizens, thinking of my own,
your rights and their protection
now we've to leave again,
that's how I feel an alien
in exile from myself, come home!

European Epitaphs

1. Hôtel Beaubourg

'*Paris change…*'
Charles Baudelaire

What with the quickly flowing Seine
a muddy snow-melt flood,
there's no more sleeping under bridges
in the shadow of Notre Dame;
so cold, it is, gargoyles spit ice,
the scent of urine and Gitanes
washed away by years, by the swollen Seine;
but those rough sleepers, they remain
though I'm no longer with them
in, for example, Rue du Temple
bundled up on a cardboard mattress,
dans le Métro, or the pouring rain—
as if what a lifetime changes,
it changes and yet keeps the same.

2. Crepuscules

in memory of Geoff Ellis

There's something about the light this morning
I wouldn't have wanted you to miss—
as when twin towers' and stained glass windows'
ashen stone was tinted rose
briefly in a dusk at Paris,

or the storm-light round a café awning
tormented by late squalls in the Marais...
No, I wouldn't have wanted you to miss

today's dawn, like a shepherd's warning;
it sweeps low clouds of purple-grey
across those higher white ones
tinted pink too by the sun's
emergence behind scratched, bending boughs
with turquoise patches and some blues...
No, I wouldn't have wanted you to miss this.

3. Airgraphs

Caught by a flak-pocked European sky,
one blacked out, overcast in fear,
when only a boy I would imagine
as if it were a love affair
my father in the Westland 'Lizzie'
his mother hadn't let him fly;

but there were peaches, pears and grapes
'somewhere in Sicily' in '43
and reading your airgraphs, dad, what I see
is a steel helmet 'always full' of lemons.

Your memories, then, would tease me out
from a fed imagination, drawn
despite the stony smell of death
at village-square memorials
because they too, the martyred dead,
had the mind of Europe in their bones.

4. Strayed Identities

Through lemon trees and jasmine
to this breezy patio
reports far in the distance
sound nearer than they are
above the background crackles
of crescendo-ing cicadas;
a train hoots off towards Murcia
and there are sharp explosions,
fireworks, or bird-scarer
carried to us here…

Although what's carrying farther
is a grief, first loss then anger,
sudden, and in need of nursing –
its voices like those for a child
sent to bed at eight o'clock
sounding as remote and near
as the trains to Murcia…
for now I lie here like that child
exiled from the conversation,
wide awake, and cursing.

5. Norway Foam

for Charles Ivan Armstrong

Out for some air on a farther shore
past homes restored to pristine whiteness,
bargeboard houses in Kristiansand,
I hear gulls' raucous morning chorus.
Haven glints fill each cross-street end.
Away, at last, beyond the embrace
of Tynemouth's north and south pier,

a breath from the Skagerrak bending us
by moorings and communal wharfs
to a fort that fired on the English once,
here too are shrill, exilic voices...
Hark at them, over Norway foam,
this long-imagined strand, its random
glimpses of their home from home.

6. Distressing

> 'a futile reminiscence of the Mill
> notion that everything old is good'
> Joseph Cornell

Still how the time's distressing
fissures plasterwork and paint
with hairline cracks—a craquelure
across its face, the sad allure
about historic damage, age,
and other pressing
levelers;
              myself among them,
caught by a vacant shop window,
catch-lights in my eyes,
staring at poor-finished chamfers
where shabby old utopias
moulder out the back...

'... a mistake, but not a disaster,'
is what one had to say—
like they'd suffered an acute nostalgia
for the early Seventies
when we were our own master
and only had ourselves to blame.

7. At Dieppe

Then on the harbour wall, Dieppe,
after driving through a night
to cross the European plain, non-stop,
arrived here, now, a couple's
quarrel at this Channel port
comes to seem the sum of it—
like they had never loved at all

in their doomed marriage (oh no, don't tell me)
or ruined love affair...
Dog-tiredness aggravates the quarrel,
and I can only look aghast, aware
it's better to have loved and lost
(as the poet had it)
especially when that good as hurts us all.

8. Doomed Marriage

River redoubling round to embrace them
and in different tongues construed,
the newly-married enter sunlight
beyond town bounds, on crisp-laid snow,
and dazzling hopes enliven eyes
tender to relatives as they're about to go...

Mountains fading into parlous distance,
nothing but an outline, a lacustrine sunset
or Adige and hills implied, see, love's
been driven from the better or worse
robbing them both of a promised release
in one another's tried embrace.

Threatened by currencies of words and coin
and called upon to make some reparation,
to pay again what you had paid before,
these stretches of imagination come
over love's distances none could cover,
a belated epithalamium!

9. Currency Issues

> '… mordaci velut icta ferro
> pinus aut impulsa cupressus Euro…'
> Horace, *Odes IV*, 6

But then fear-project calculations,
how they flourish their designs
when money like an antique wind,
a *lingua franca* from beyond
the Alps, now alters its direction,
comes troubling the cypresses
and gnaws at ranks of pines;

it passes on indebtedness
to bankrupt others, save its own,
and in this smoke wind raises, this
raining all the time, you know
who'll have to fund those losses
costing the here and now.

10. Divorce Bill

There's no such thing as a no-fault divorce,
even though we had one—
its two-year-long transition phase
another solitary way
to go, with all the world before us,
and a continental love-child of my own…

nor nothing doomed about that marriage,
though even now it's like an air-bridge
without a plane arrived;
but, still, here's us obliged to leave
because we never did deserve
to stay—

which is why you'll have to pay, to pay and pay.

11. In the Vicinity

remembering Charles Tomlinson

On the A34 through snow remnants and thick spray,
we're hurrying south to save a few minutes
when at Stoke his Maastricht was our Austerlitz
comes echoing back in the last streaks of day;
and whatever *Any Questions* panelists might say
about this political year come to bits…
the lost time… our deepened austerities, it's
hard to imagine how they'll ever get away
from the blue yonder promises or what scope
there'd be for being kind, cruel to be kind,

tough on its causes, and how they may cope
with that certain disappointment when you find
(not having the aid of a neighbour Europe)
leaving, we'll be further left behind.

12. Wintering Gulls

What with our latest chilly spells,
austerities, how the seagulls
this far inland patrol crisped lawn
as if coming into their own.
They buzz the part-refurbished library's
smooth grey cladding overhead
screened by a half-baked slogan:
IN A WORLD OF GREY BE RED
Be red, old brick, old red brick walls!

But this one, it flaps at the well read
strolling past some street-food shacks.
It grabs scraps, mocks those words'
witless unrealities; it attacks,
drives off the other flustered birds,
its yellow-angled beak, steel eyes
hurtled from a clouded, ill-fed,
greyed world seeing red
and, my goodness, how it cries!

13. What's Left

for Adam Piette

Starting from the earliest
terrace on this hillside,
it's all downhill from here
and reassuring, solid
house-fronts line the way
to a scheduled train by way
of some more stubborn British art—
like Spencer's *Helter Skelter*
or a Bomberg Spanish landscape
for instance, with this strange,
estranging afterlife
on wooded, green expanses
and Parkhill frieze of flats;
they're holding steadfast, steady,
as if composed before me
like a swan-song for what's left.

14. An Evening's Red

Just think then: clouds in a sunset
diffusing red-rimmed light
might comment on the pressed commuters
taken backwards down these lines
enclosed in the green, Great Western,
nostalgic livery.

This charged dusk tone at springtime
flashes equivocal signs
off west-facing windows

on trackside glass developments
sandwiched in between failed firms'
whitewashed brick façades…

It grants an odd solidity
to hillside grass and copse;
then goes, as if this edge of Europe's
Cimmerian, sunset lands
were bringing down the curtain
on all our misplaced hopes.

15. England in 2019

Even as the hollyhocks will still grow tall,
lattice-work fencing need to be replaced,
bottle banks choke, the rose petals fall
across walls double-edged graffiti has defaced,
still the people's will will have been done
and dusted, somehow, rain, it will still rain
from storm-clouds upon our fainting country, sun
pick out brick courses, into the bargain.
From a muddy spring, the mud will invite them,
rulers, managing interminable wars,
to reverse engineer a continental system—
spiting faces, beggaring the neighbours…
Then, as deficits mount, some phantom may
burst to illumine our chilly, real day.

Colouring the Past

'do recollect—that all is at stake—'
Lord Byron, 5 February 1816

At overcast Easter, down Mather Avenue,
the late buds nipped on branches,
our changing climate's come to this:
though spring is here to me
it's colouring the past, lost times
revalued in this after-light.

Remember, despite my ruined smile,
the post-op trauma and lost face,
she let me sleep beside her
one last night in our marriage bed;
and I had dreamed we could stay friends
despite the falling out of love—
some hope, missed chance, some hope!

Then this is what they'd have to mean,
that framed *Last Judgment* on the wall
or else a map of Europe
with its countries' varied colours,
'my heart drawn taut between them'
and 'the colouring of the past'
from which no word would reach
bringing our house down, stone by stone,
above the lake, beyond an arch,
its ruins overgrown...

Yet still that silenced conversation
would have to be continued,
as through cross-Channel marriages
differences are held in common
and not to mention deadlocked deeds,
the flooded gutters, puddled verges'
petrol rainbows interfused,
its weed-fouled frontage with a door
which swings now onto nothing—

onto nothing after near fifty years.

Haus Europe

'… Ere their story die.'
Thomas Hardy

for Matty and Raphael

Bluish in a white-out light at dawn,
snow blowing through a streetlamp's nimbus
was more nostalgia for our Cold War
where the ghost of a family car
hunkered beside iced-over pine fronds
shivering at an east wind's
sudden return to winter that mid-March.

But here in the Alps at an end of winter
by heaped-up strata, smutty snow,
last night a hungry deer
fed from the garden's dry grass ends
while glasses sounding for our health
mixed dialect, language, idiom
from south and north, come home;

and now this sound of distant gunfire
or—as likely—rolling thunder
is a starting avalanche
under the town band's foreground tones
scaring off its grown-up young ones,
who would be compelled to leave
resounding bands of rock, pines, chalets'
shuttered windows under eaves
piled high with layered snow.

Back then dawn silence stunned the air,
but for one far jet-engine roar;
an inbound flight from somewhere,
it was our European lovers
needing their own safe place to land;
and the few tracks in that roadway's snow
stood out as worry furrows
on their brows, each pining for the other!
Then, like those who neither feel nor know,
if we can't help them live and move,
well, there again, it's time to say no more…

Postcards from Bern

1

Given my vertigo, wish you were here,
while loved ones climbed the cathedral spire
and I listen to a street musician
lift the spirits higher—
bringing those *Recuerdos* of the Alhambra
to Münsterplatz at Bern.

2

The wood scents from a church interior
call up Scargill's V-shaped chapel.
I'm catching my breath by its graveyard at Thun.
Away across the lake
an echo of Von Kleist's last cry
couldn't shift a cloud above
our young couple's sky.

3

In rose-flush sunset on still whitened peaks
of the Bernese Oberland
by opened windows, were you looking down
from what feels like a Ferris wheel's height,
thanks to Robert Walser's footprints in the snow
or those few marks on some paper by Paul Klee,
this illuminating town
might go the distance to disprove
what Harry Lime *would* say.

4

Had you been here, it seems only right
a balloon should rise above Monbijou
as if lifting off towards the Baltic Sea's
beaches on the day we leave—
and, were you, it might climb up to disprove
disparaging of all the peaceful arts can do
with their grown-fonder love,
or your memories.

Empty Vase

also for O

1

That empty vase in a front window bay,
vase with blue willow-pattern lines,
it's missing a birth- or a Valentine's day
for us to have our rare designs
upon its inner emptiness, that vase
come from a junk, no, a charity shop
where I'll have paid a tiny sum
on a nondescript autumn afternoon
to take its vacancy away.

2

Though forgotten in such emptiness
long winters long, still, it serves to say
of all the infinite times or places
in which two might have moved and loved,
oh no, you didn't miss each other,
for here it was we coincided—
communicating through these times of ours,
and like that vase were a momentary stay
waiting for its complements of flowers.

Notes

BELONGINGS: The epigraph ('The days go by I remain') is part of the refrain to Guillaume Apollinaire's 'Le pont Mirabeau' from his first book *Alcools* (1914).

MONTEROSSO: The resort on the Ligurian coast where Eugenio Montale's family owned a villa. Quotations from his early poem 'I limoni' (The Lemon Trees) and others are painted on the town's walls. His epigraph to section three imagines contemporary writers: '… located in the history of our Country, which doesn't exclude them from being European citizens.'

WRITTEN IN THE BAY: The epigraph is the end of 'Lines Written in the Bay of Lerici', a late poems in which the exact wording of the final couplet is conjectured by Shelley's editors.

LINCOLNSHIRE LANDSCAPES: The epigraph is from Richard Wollheim's review in *The Listener* of *Problems of the Self: Philosophical Papers 1956–1972* (1973) by Bernard Williams.

BALKAN TRILOGY: The title is from Olivia Manning's sequence of novels, and the epigraph is from Vittorio Sereni's 'Diaro d'Algeria' poem about the D-Day Landings. Geoffrey Hill voted 'remain' in the 2016 referendum, as suggested by the first section's epigraph from his 1998 poem.

GARDEN THOUGHTS: The epigraph is from 'Quartiere Solari' in *L'ippopotamo* (1989).

BIBLIOGRAPHICAL NOTE: The epigraph is from 'In der Fremde' (In a Foreign Land). Derek Slade is the bibliographer of the poet Roy Fisher (1930–2017).

IN THE APENNINES: Eric Newby's *Love and War in the Apennines* (1971) relates how between summer 1943 and January 1944 he was hidden in mountains above Parma, returning to marry the young woman who, for some six months, had helped him evade capture.

PLAZA DE LAS MONJAS: Antonio Orihuela organizes the *Voces del estremo* festival in Juan Ramón Jiménez's birthplace. The epigraph from 'Un fantasma recorre Europa…' reads 'we quickly close the frontier… A phantom runs through Europe.' The square flanks a nunnery, hence its name.

OUT OF EUROPE: The epigraph is from William Empson's 'Aubade'.

SONNING LOCK: In 1611 this famous remark caused Sir Henry Wotton a temporary disgrace.

DIE HOLZWEGE: The title is a term of Heidegger's meaning 'The Wood-Ways', the epigraph from Nietzsche's *Nachgelassene Fragmente*, autumn 1887, and reads 'the eye of the nihilist… is unfaithful to his memories—it allows them to drop, to lose their leaves'.

NIGHT FLIGHT: The close of James Joyce's 'The Dead' provides the epigraph. Other allusions to it, to Yeats' 'Sailing to Byzantium', and Marvell's 'Horatian Ode' colour the final stanza.

WHERE EUROPE ENDS: The title alludes to Yoko Tawada's story 'Where Europe Begins', whose last phrase ('I noticed I was standing in the middle of Europe') is cited as the epigraph to section two. Conrad wrote from Singapore on 13 October 1885 that 'When speaking, writing or thinking in English the word Home always means for me the hospitable shores of Great Britain.' In 'Nel cimitero di Chiswick', Salvatore Quasimodo expressed the view that 'L'amore per le ombre foscoliane è piú qui / che in Santa Croce' ('Love for the shades of Foscolo is more present here / than in Santa Croce'). In 1871 the exiled poet's remains were removed to the Florentine church where they now reside.

THE FURTHER LOSSES: The historian Christopher Duggan (1957–2015), whose death partly inspired this sequence and with whom the signed editions are exchanged in 'After Poussin' is the author of *The Force of Destiny: A History of Italy since 1798* (2007). The epigraph is from the Brazilian poet's 'Aurora' in *Brejo das almas* (1934).

SAUDADES DA EUROPA: Tabucci provides definitions of the Portuguese word 'saudade', from which the first lines of each stanza are adapted, in *Viaggi e altri viaggi* (2010).

LAST REFUGE: According to Boswell, Dr. Johnson remarked that 'Patriotism is the last refuge of a scoundrel' on 7 April 1775. Bob Dylan embroidered it in the fifth verse to his 'Sweetheart Like You', released on the *Infidels* album in 1983.

COLD COMFORT: This epigraph is the final line to Saba's poem from *Parole* (1933–34).

WALL-TO-WALL: The Dutch Embassy in Sofia initiated the 'Wall-to-wall' poetry project in 2004, choosing 'So I believe that also you are' by Jan Hanlo (1912–1969) for the back wall of the Natural History Museum. Cees Nooteboom's remark is the headline to an article on his *Tumbas: tombe di poeti e pensatori,* a book on the tombs of poets and thinkers.

DON QUIXOTE IN SOFIA: The epigraph, from Chapter 6 of *Don Quixote,* fears that, once cured of his illusions, the hero might 'turn poet, for that disease is incurable and catching' (J. M. Cohen's translation). This poem was prompted by two paintings in the National Gallery, Sofia.

THE IRISH BORDER: The epigraph is from 'Rita Duffy: *Watchtower II*' in *One Thousand Things Worth Knowing* (2015).

ON THE ELECTRICITY: The phrases are from Alexander Shurbanov's 'All the Immortality We Have' in *Foresun* (2016) and Peter Riley's version of 'Lines on the Unknown Soldier'. The third quatrain remembers the final stanza to W. H. Auden's 'September 1, 1939'.

LEAVE TO REMAIN: The epigraph is from 'Die Behörde' (The Competent Authority) and means 'as non-existent in the stubborn sense of bourgeois convention'.

HÔTEL BEAUBOURG: The epigraph is from Baudelaire's 'Le cygne'. I first visited Paris, without the funds for a hotel room, in October 1970.

DISTRESSING: Joseph Cornell wrote these words in his journal on 11 November 1967, to be found in *Theater of the Mind: Selected Diaries, Letters, and Files* ed. Mary Ann Caws (2001).

CURRENCY ISSUES: The epigraph reads 'pine struck by cutting iron or cypress felled by the Euro'. The 'Euro', as it appears in Horace and in Montale's 'Il ventaglio' from *La bufera e altro* (1957), was then the Roman name for a southeast wind bringing storms.

IN THE VICINITY: Charles Tomlinson (1927–2015), a poet born in Stoke-on-Trent whose work I admire, would probably, had be been living, have voted 'leave' in the 2016 referendum—if the phrase half-remembered from his 'Napoleon' (which reads 'Maastricht / was the Waterloo we lost, a diplomatic/Austerlitz') is anything to go by.

HAUS EUROPE: The epigraph is the final line to 'In Time of "the Breaking of Nations"'.

Acknowledgements

Many of the poems in *Ravishing Europa* have appeared, sometimes in earlier versions, in the following places: 'Belongings' was first published in *The English Association Newsletter*, August 2016, and then with 'Violated landscape', Strayed Identities' and 'Out of Europe' in *Poetry Salzburg Review* 30 (Winter 2016–17). 'Monterosso' was included in *Noon: Journal of the Short Poem* no. 12, October 2016. 'Written in the Bay' and 'Divorce Bill' appeared in the University of Reading *Creative Arts Anthology* for 2018. 'Balkan Trilogy' appeared in a Geoffrey Hill memorial issue of *Agenda* in September 2016. *Shearsman Magazine* (Spring 2017) published 'Ravishing Europa', 'Garden Thoughts', 'Bibliographical Footnote' and 'Lincolnshire Landscapes'. 'Belongings', 'Balkan Trilogy', 'Lincolnshire Landscapes' and 'Post-Truth' also featured in an online publication called *Brexit and the Democratic Intellect* (University of Durham, 2017). 'Plaza de las Monjas' appeared alongside its translation into Spanish by Conrado Santamaría and Amalia García Fuertes in *Voces del estremo: Anthologia 2012–2016* ed. Antonio Orihuela (Amargord ediciones) in July 2017. A revised version was published in the *Notre Dame Review* no. 46 (July 2018). 'On a Walk to Sonning' and 'World Citizens' were both published in *The High Window* No. 8 (Winter 2017). 'The Prospects' was first published in *Raceme* no. 6 (April 2018). 'Sonning Lock' and 'What's Left' were published in *The Interpreter's House* no. 65 (Summer 2017) and the latter in the Introduction to *Stanley Spencer Poems: An Anthology* (Two Rivers Press, 2017). 'Die Holzwege' was written for *The Tree Line: Poems for Trees, Woods & People* ed. Michael McKimm (Worple Press, 2017). 'Night Flight' appeared in the *Irish Times*, Saturday 21 October 2017. 'Post-Truth' also appeared with 'Drawing a Line' in the University of Reading *Creative Arts Anthology* for 2017.

'Where Europe Ends' was written for *Wretched Strangers*, an anthology edited by Agnes Lehoczky and J. T. Welsch (Boiler House Press and UEA, 2018). 'Last Refuge', 'In the Vicinity' and 'Wintering Gulls' appeared in *Poetry Salzburg Review* no. 33 (November 2018). 'On the Electricity' was first reproduced in *Molly Bloom* 13 as part of a section dedicated to the memory of Roy Fisher and Tom Raworth. 'Distressing' was published in *Tears in the Fence* no. 38, summer 2018. Nine of the 'European Epitaphs' were published in *Blackbox Manifold* 20 (July 2018). 'Empty Vase' appeared in the April / May 2018 issue of *The London Magazine*. 'The Further Losses', 'Night Flight', 'Drawing a Line', 'Post-Truth', 'Die Holzwege', 'Divorce Bill', and 'Written in the Bay' were published online in *The Fortnightly Review* (2018). 'Bloomsbury Way' and 'The Hard and Soft of It' appeared in *English* (Winter 2018). My gratitude and thanks go to the editors of all the above.